Blastoff! Readers are carefully developed by literacy experts to build reading stamina and move students toward fluency by combining standards-based content with developmentally appropriate text.

 Level 1 provides the most support through repetition of high-frequency words, light text, predictable sentence patterns, and strong visual support.

 Level 2 offers early readers a bit more challenge through varied sentences, increased text load, and text-supportive special features.

 Level 3 advances early-fluent readers toward fluency through increased text load, less reliance on photos, advancing concepts, longer sentences, and more complex special features.

★ **Blastoff! Universe**

This edition first published in 2026 by Bellwether Media, Inc.

No part of this publication may be reproduced in whole or in part without written permission of the publisher. For information regarding permission, write to Bellwether Media, Inc., Attention: Permissions Department, 3500 American Blvd W, Suite 150, Bloomington, MN 55431.

Library of Congress Cataloging-in-Publication Data

LC record for Malaysia available at: https://lccn.loc.gov/2025015024

Text copyright © 2026 by Bellwether Media, Inc. BLASTOFF! READERS and associated logos are trademarks and/or registered trademarks of Bellwether Media, Inc. Bellwether Media is a division of FlutterBee Education Group.

Editor: Betsy Rathburn   Designer: Laura Sowers

Printed in the United States of America, North Mankato, MN.

Table of Contents

All About Malaysia	4
Land and Animals	6
Life in Malaysia	12
Malaysia Facts	20
Glossary	22
To Learn More	23
Index	24

All About Malaysia

Kuala Lumpur

Malaysia is a country in Southeast Asia. One part is on a **peninsula**. The other is on an island.

Malaysia has lively cities. Kuala Lumpur is the capital.

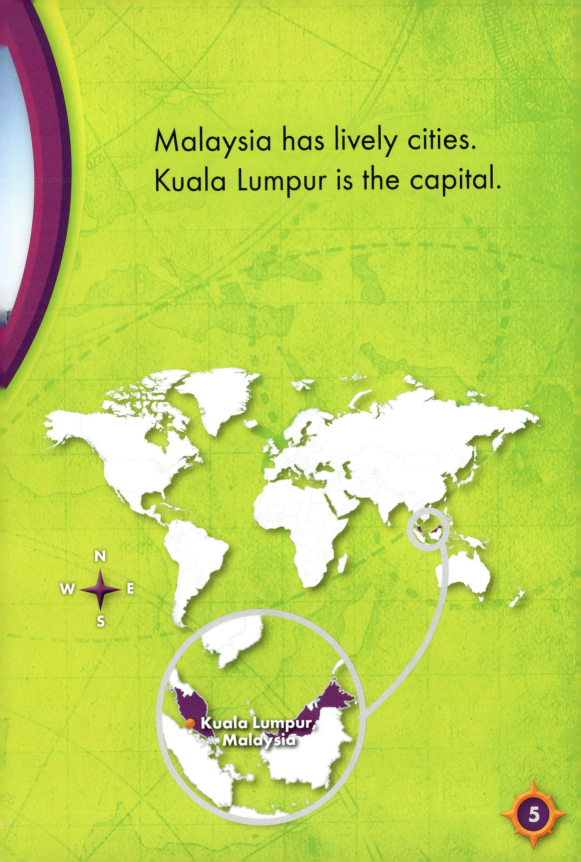

Land and Animals

Coastal plains rise into hills and mountains. Thick **rain forests** cover much of the country.

Mountain rivers empty into **tropical** seas. Many islands lie off the coasts.

rain forest

Mount Kinabalu

Size: 13,435 feet (4,095 meters) tall
Famous For: highest mountain in Malaysia

Malaysia is tropical. It is hot and **humid** all year. It is cooler in the mountains.

Monsoons bring rain throughout the year.

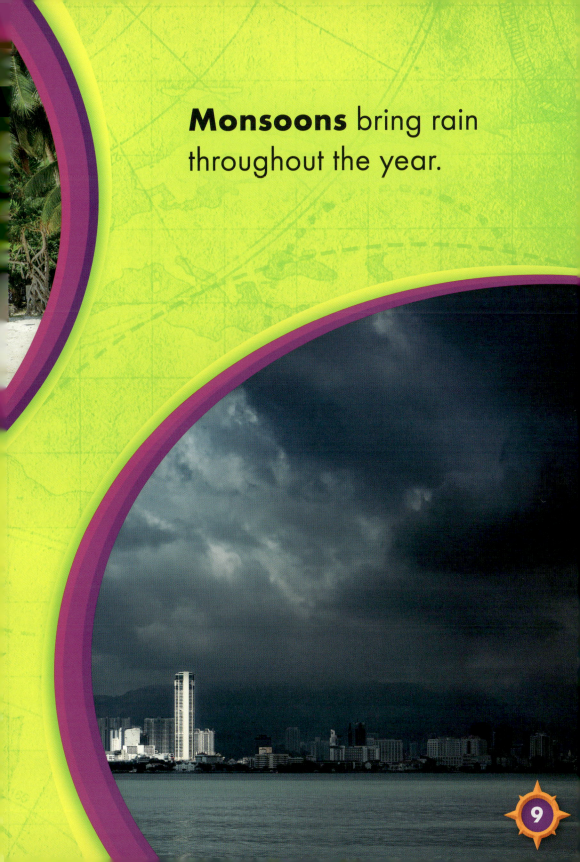

Orangutans swing from trees. Hornbills fly overhead. Elephants feed in forests and **grasslands**.

Asian elephants

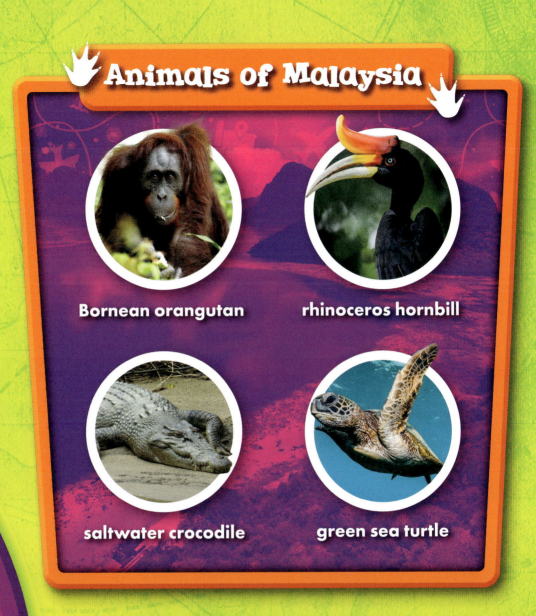

Crocodiles hunt in **mangroves**. Sea turtles lay eggs on beaches.

Life in Malaysia

Around half of Malaysians have a Malay **background**. Most people are **Muslims**.

Malay is the main language. Many people also speak English.

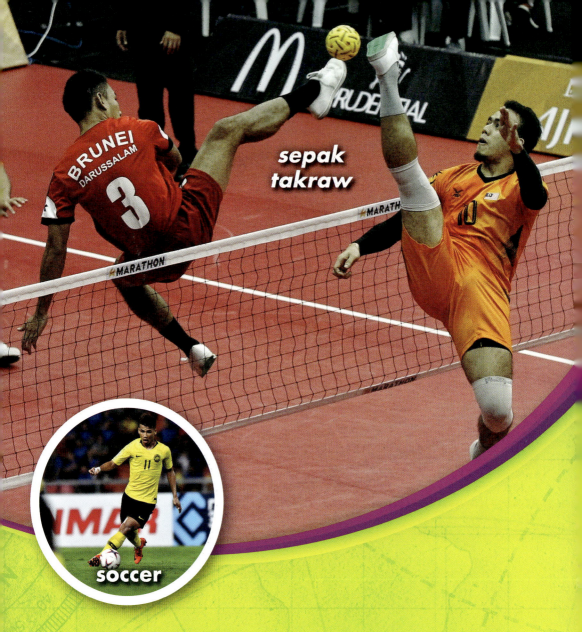

Soccer is the most popular sport. *Sepak takraw* is also common. Players hit a ball over a net with their feet.

Some people visit beaches. Others explore cities and parks!

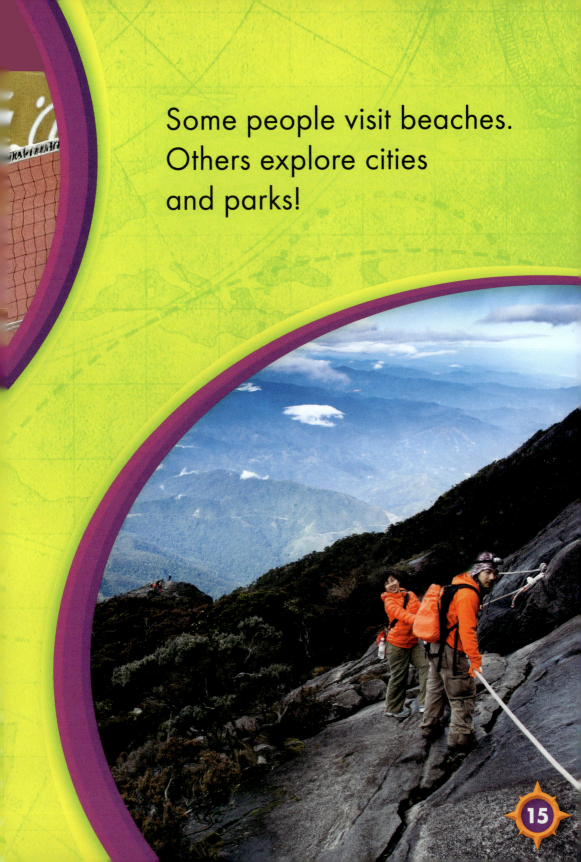

Nasi lemak is rice cooked in coconut milk. *Mee goreng* is a fried noodle dish.

Malaysian Foods

nasi lemak

mee goreng

roti john

fried bananas

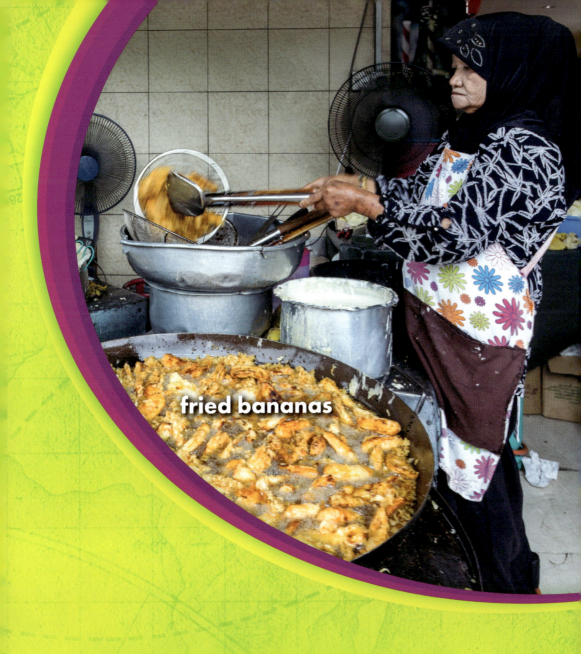
fried bananas

Roti john is a sandwich with egg and meat. Fried bananas are a treat!

Muslims fast and pray during Ramadan. People **celebrate** Chinese New Year for 15 days.

Diwali is an important **festival** for **Hindus**. Malaysians enjoy festivals all year long!

Diwali

Chinese New Year

Malaysia Facts

Size:
127,355 square miles
(329,847 square kilometers)

Population:
34,564,810 (2024)

National Holiday:
Independence Day (August 31)

Main Language:
Malay

Capital City:
Kuala Lumpur

Famous Face

Name: Michelle Yeoh

Famous For: award-winning actress

Religions

- Hindu: 6%
- other: 3%
- Christian: 9%
- Buddhist: 19%
- Muslim: 63%

Top Landmarks

Batu Caves

Gunung Mulu National Park

Petronas Twin Towers

Glossary

background—people's experiences, knowledge, and family history

celebrate—to do something special or fun for an event, occasion, or holiday

coastal plains—areas of flat land with few trees that lie next to the ocean

festival—a time or event of celebration

grasslands—lands covered with grasses and other soft plants with few bushes or trees

Hindus—people who follow Hinduism; Hinduism is a religion that began in India.

humid—having a lot of water in the air

mangroves—thick tropical forests that can grow along coasts in salty water

monsoons—winds that shift direction each season; monsoons bring heavy rain.

Muslims—people of the Islamic faith; Muslims follow the teachings of the Prophet Muhammad as told to him from Allah.

peninsula—a part of the land that sticks out from a larger piece of land and is almost completely surrounded by water

rain forests—thick, green forests that receive a lot of rain

tropical—having to do with a place that is hot and wet

To Learn More

AT THE LIBRARY

Gregory, Joy. *Malaysia*. New York, N.Y.: Lightbox Learning Inc., 2025.

Kington, Emily. *Orangutans*. Cornwall, U.K.: Hungry Tomato, 2022.

Sabelko, Rebecca. *Singapore*. Minneapolis, Minn.: Bellwether Media, 2025.

ON THE WEB

FACTSURFER

Factsurfer.com gives you a safe, fun way to find more information.

1. Go to www.factsurfer.com.

2. Enter "Malaysia" into the search box and click 🔍.

3. Select your book cover to see a list of related content.

Index

animals, 10, 11
beaches, 11, 15
capital (see Kuala Lumpur)
Chinese New Year, 18, 19
cities, 5, 15
coastal plains, 6
Diwali, 18
English, 12
food, 16, 17
forests, 10
grasslands, 10
hills, 6
Hindus, 18
island, 4, 6
Kuala Lumpur, 4, 5
Malay, 12, 13
Malaysia facts, 20-21
mangroves, 11
map, 5
monsoons, 9
Mount Kinabalu, 7

mountains, 6, 7, 8
Muslims, 12, 18
peninsula, 4
people, 12, 14, 15, 18
rain forests, 6
Ramadan, 18
rivers, 6
say hello, 13
sepak takraw, 14
soccer, 14
Southeast Asia, 4

The images in this book are reproduced through the courtesy of: Igor Plotnikov, front cover; Mini Onion, pp. 4-5; SeanPavonePhoto, pp. 3, 21 (Petronas Twin Towers); Arnain, p. 6; alenthien, pp. 6-7; Kjersti, pp. 8-9; hafizanwar, p. 9; Chaiphorn, pp. 10-11; Daniel Lamborn, p. 11 (Bornean orangutan); Jamil Bin Mat Isa, p. 11 (rhinoceros hornbill); Christian Lehmann, p. 11 (saltwater crocodile); Aaron, p. 11 (green sea turtle); FAROQ, p. 12; Ng Kok Beng, pp. 12-13; almonfoto, p. 14 (soccer); Mohd Nasirruddin Yazid, pp. 14-15; Tappasan Phurisamrit, p. 15; WONG SZE FEI, p. 16 (*nasi lemak*); akulamatiau, p. 16 (*mee goreng*); azami, p. 16 (*roti john*); doucefleur, p. 16 (fried bananas); Stanley Cabigas/ Alamy Stock Photo, p. 17; Natalia Milko/ Alamy Stock Photo, p. 18; gracethang, pp. 18-19; Zerbor, p. 20 (flag); Image Press Agency/ Alamy Stock Photo, p. 20 (Michelle Yeoh); Richie Chan, p. 21 (Batu Caves); MICHEL, p. 21 (Gunung Mulu National Park); SanchaiRat, p. 23.